TENNESSEE TITANS

by Charlie Beattie

Abdo & Daughters
MIDDLE GRADE NONFICTION

An imprint of Abdo Publishing
abdobooks.com

Published by Abdo Publishing, a division of ABDO, PO Box 398166, Minneapolis, Minnesota 55439.
Copyright © 2026 by Abdo Consulting Group, Inc. International copyrights reserved in all countries.
No part of this book may be reproduced in any form without written permission from the publisher.
Abdo & Daughters™ is a trademark and logo of Abdo Publishing.

Printed in China.
052025
092025

THIS BOOK CONTAINS RECYCLED MATERIALS

Cover Photos: Quinn Harris/Getty Images Sport/Getty Images (Jeffery Simmons); George Gojkovich/
Getty Images Sport/Getty Images (Warren Moon)
Interior Photos: Cooper Neill/Getty Images Sport/Getty Images, 4–5, 6, 57, 59; Aaron M. Sprecher/AP
Images, 7; Carmen Mandato/Getty Images Sport/Getty Images, 8; Gray Quetti/Cal Sport Media/AP
Images, 9; Abdo Publishing, 10–11; AP Images, 12–13, 18, 26, 31, 60 (top); Ed Kolenovsky/AP Images, 14,
25; David F. Smith/AP Images, 15; Richard Stagg/Getty Images Sport/Getty Images, 16; Focus on Sport/
Getty Images, 17; Charles Aqua Viva/Getty Images Sport/Getty Images, 19; Al Messerschmidt Archive/
AP Images, 21, 28, 50; Richard Mackson/Sports Illustrated/Getty Images, 22–23, 60 (bottom); Michael
Zagaris/Getty Images Sport/Getty Images, 24; Focus on Sport/Getty Images Sport/Getty Images, 27,
33, 40; David Nance/Houston Chronicle/AP Images, 29; Diamond Images/Getty Images, 30; George
Gojkovich/Getty Images Sport/Getty Images, 34–35, 39; Tom DiPace/AP Images, 36, 63; Owen C.
Shaw/Getty Images Sport/Getty Images, 37; Chuck Solomon/AP Images, 38; Donna Bagby/AP Images,
42; Rick Stewart/Allsport/Getty Images Sport/Getty Images, 43; Jake Herrle/AP Images, 44; Doug
Pensinger/Allsport/Getty Images Sport/Getty Images, 45; Damian Strohmeyer/Sports Illustrated/Getty
Images, 46–47; Stephen Dunn/Allsport/Getty Images Sport/Getty Images, 48; Wade Payne/AP Images,
49, 61 (bottom left); Scott Audette/AP Images, 51; Icon Sportswire/Getty Images, 52; Paul Spinelli/AP
Images, 53; John Russell/AP Images, 54–55, 61 (top); Frederick Breedon/Getty Images Sport/Getty
Images, 56, 61 (bottom right); Shutterstock Images, 58

Editor: Rebecca Higgins
Series Designer: Laura Graphenteen
Production Designer: Laura Kuchar

Library of Congress Control Number: 2024948478

Publisher's Cataloging-in-Publication Data

Names: Beattie, Charlie, author.
Title: Tennessee Titans / by Charlie Beattie
Description: Minneapolis, Minnesota: Abdo Publishing, 2026 | Series: Inside the NFL | Includes online
     resources and index.
Identifiers: ISBN 9781098296926 (lib. bdg.) | ISBN 9798384919445 (ebook)
Subjects: LCSH: Tennessee Titans (Football team)--Juvenile literature. | National Football League--
     Juvenile literature. | Football teams--Juvenile literature. | American football--Juvenile literature.
Classification: DDC 796.333--dc23

CONTENTS

Tennessee Titans running back Derrick Henry looks for an opening in a game against the Houston Texans on January 3, 2021.

CHAPTER 1

RUMBLING INTO THE RECORD BOOKS

TENNESSEE TITANS RUNNING BACK DERRICK HENRY TOOK A HANDOFF from his quarterback, Ryan Tannehill, and surged forward. A Houston Texans defender tried to wrap Henry up at the line of scrimmage. The running back blasted through the tackle and continued to churn his legs. By the time Houston defensive end Jonathan Greenard had pulled down the 247-pound running back, Henry had gained 8 tough yards.

It was Week 17 of the 2020 National Football League (NFL) season. The Titans needed a win over Houston to secure the American Football Conference (AFC) South division title. But the league's biggest running back had another goal in mind. He was 223 rushing yards shy of 2,000 for the season. Reaching that mark wouldn't only help Henry's team, it would also

Henry, *right*, was named the NFL's Offensive Player of the Year after the 2020 season.

make him just the eighth runner in the 100-year history of the NFL to top 2,000.

WORKHORSE

Henry was an interesting prospect coming out of college. He had won the Heisman Trophy as college football's best player in 2015, but not everyone considered him to be a sure NFL star. At Alabama, Henry often used his size to run over defenders. But scouts wondered if he could take on the bigger, faster defenders in the NFL. When the Titans picked Henry in the second round of the 2016 draft, some NFL experts considered it a big mistake.

Henry eventually proved doubters wrong. He became the team's starting back in 2018 and rushed for 1,059 yards and 12 touchdowns. The next season, he led the NFL with 1,540 yards and 16 scores. Entering 2020, Henry had established himself as one of the league's best rushers.

In recent history, NFL teams have avoided wearing out their running backs by limiting their carries. But Tennessee knew Henry could handle more work. He carried the ball a league-high 303 times in 2019. Entering his Week 17 showdown with the Texans, Henry had taken 334 handoffs in 2020.

BUSTING LOOSE

After one quarter of play, the chances of Henry reaching 2,000 yards didn't look great. He still needed 203 more yards. But the first play of the second quarter changed everything.

Tennessee lined up on second-and-two at its own 48. Henry took the handoff and followed the right side of his offensive line. Spotting a small hole, he burst

Henry breaks away for a 52-yard run in the second quarter against Houston.

through it just before Houston's J. J. Watt could get a hand on him. Looking up, he spotted two more Texans' tacklers. With a slight juke to his left, Henry cut back and left them both behind. The big back outraced everyone to the end zone for a 52-yard score.

Suddenly, Henry was closer to making history. Tennessee's

Henry rushed for more than 200 yards in a game three times during the 2020 season.

coaches kept feeding him the ball. After Henry broke five tackles on a hard-charging 45-yard run with 5:41 left in the third quarter, the running back was closing in on 2,000 rushing yards.

Houston scored again with just 10:14 left in the game to take a 35–31 lead. Though winning the game was more important than their running back's milestone, the Titans knew Henry was their best path to victory. Tennessee put together a 20-play drive that took nearly nine minutes. Henry carried the ball eight times. On his third run of the drive, he took a handoff at the Titans' 45 and dragged two tacklers for 6 yards. That amazing run put him over the 2,000 mark.

The Titans finished that long drive with a touchdown to take a 38–35 lead. And though Houston drove to tie the game, the Titans still had time to answer. Henry's final carry of the day went for 4 yards and set up the game-winning 37-yard field goal. Henry finished the game with 34 carries, a career-high 250 rushing yards, and two touchdowns. Thanks to a monster performance from the NFL's most feared rusher, the Titans secured the division title.

MR. 2,000

Though Derrick Henry fell short of the NFL record for yards in a season in 2020, he made his own mark on football history. Henry rushed for more than 2,000 yards four times in high school. He then rushed for 2,215 during his final year at Alabama. After his performance in 2020, he became the first running back to ever break the 2,000-yard barrier at all three levels of football.

During Henry's senior season of high school in Yulee, Florida, he rushed for 4,261 yards and 55 touchdowns.

NFL TEAMS MAP

NFC

NFC EAST
 DALLAS COWBOYS
 NEW YORK GIANTS
 PHILADELPHIA EAGLES
 WASHINGTON COMMANDERS

NFC WEST
 ARIZONA CARDINALS
 LOS ANGELES RAMS
 SAN FRANCISCO 49ERS
 SEATTLE SEAHAWKS

NFC NORTH
 CHICAGO BEARS
 DETROIT LIONS
 GREEN BAY PACKERS
 MINNESOTA VIKINGS

NFC SOUTH
 ATLANTA FALCONS
 CAROLINA PANTHERS
 NEW ORLEANS SAINTS
 TAMPA BAY BUCCANEERS

AFC

AFC EAST	AFC WEST	AFC NORTH	AFC SOUTH
BUFFALO BILLS	DENVER BRONCOS	BALTIMORE RAVENS	HOUSTON TEXANS
MIAMI DOLPHINS	KANSAS CITY CHIEFS	CINCINNATI BENGALS	INDIANAPOLIS COLTS
NEW ENGLAND PATRIOTS	LAS VEGAS RAIDERS	CLEVELAND BROWNS	JACKSONVILLE JAGUARS
NEW YORK JETS	LOS ANGELES CHARGERS	PITTSBURGH STEELERS	TENNESSEE TITANS

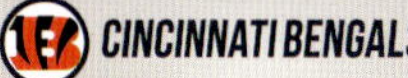

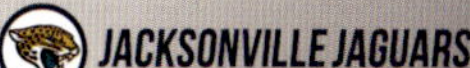

Bud Adams, *left*, helped create the American Football League (AFL) in 1960.

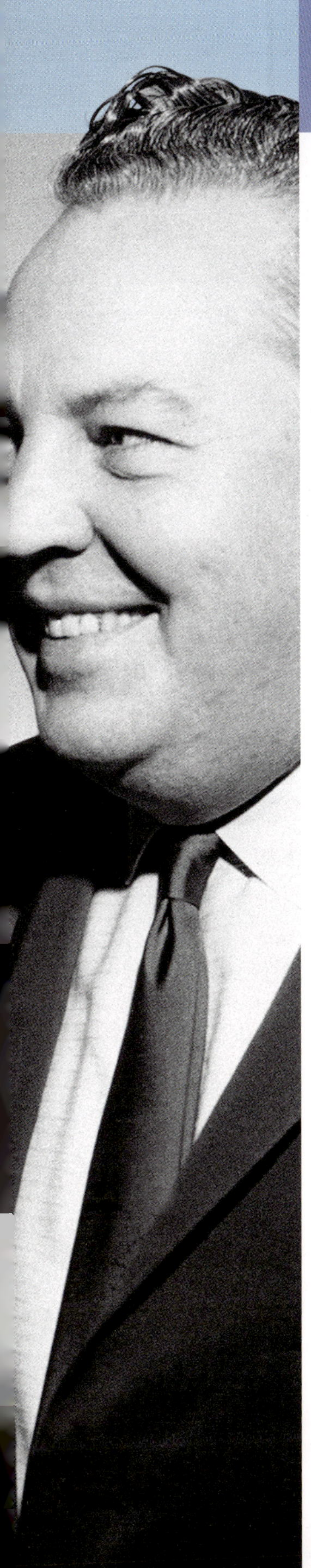

CHAPTER 2

AN INSTANT DYNASTY

MORE PEOPLE THAN EVER WERE WATCHING THE NFL IN THE LATE 1950s. While baseball remained the United States' most popular sport at the time, football was quickly catching up. At the end of the decade, the NFL had 12 teams. But a handful of potential owners wanted in.

One of them was Bud Adams, who had made a fortune in the oil business. For years, he had been trying to get a team for his hometown of Houston. However, his attempts to acquire an NFL expansion team had never gotten very far. In 1959, he changed his tactics. Adams joined forces with other would-be NFL owners, such as Dallas's Lamar Hunt and Buffalo's Ralph Wilson. The group of eight investors formed a new pro football league. Calling themselves "the Foolish Club," they founded the

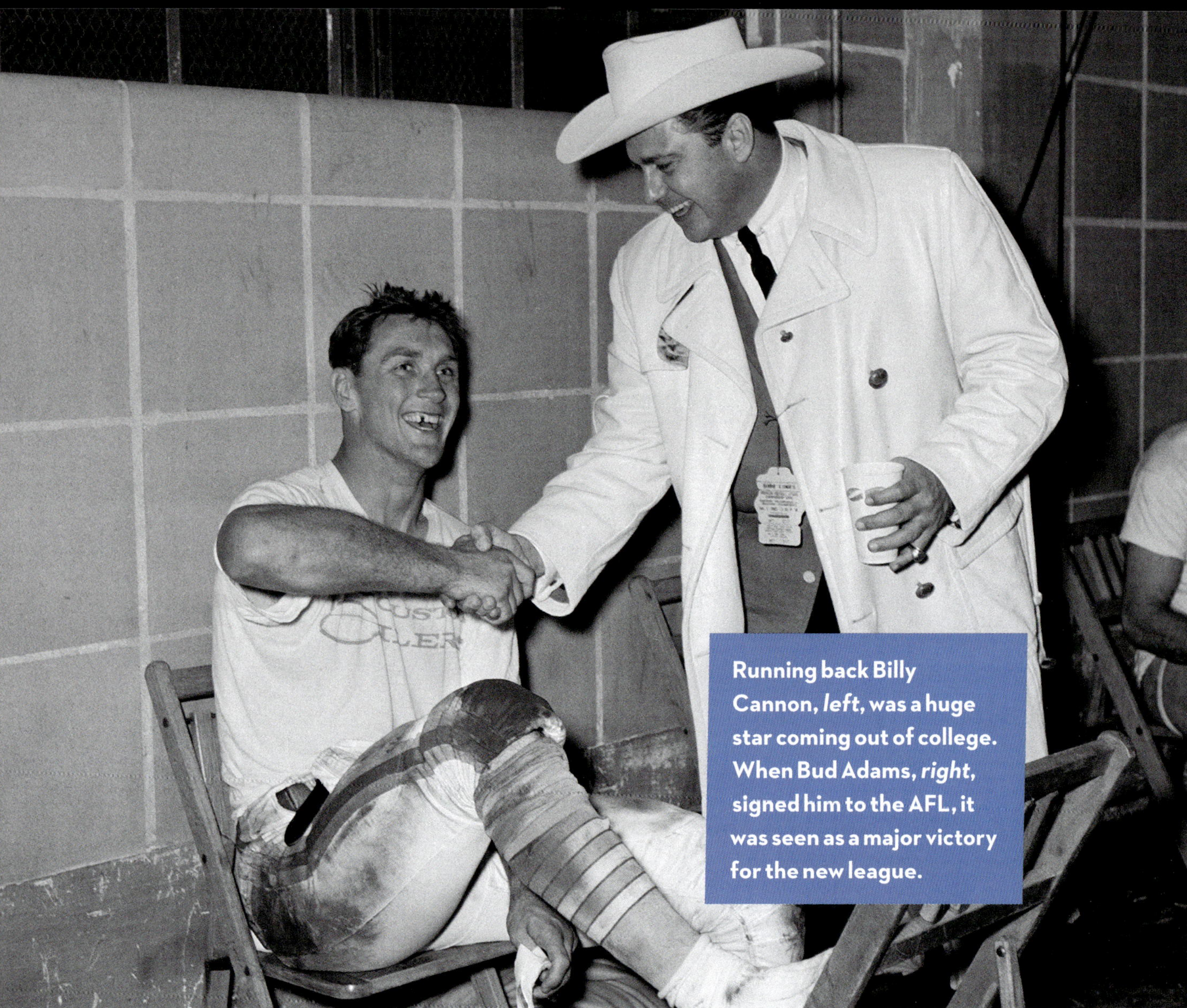

Running back Billy Cannon, *left*, was a huge star coming out of college. When Bud Adams, *right*, signed him to the AFL, it was seen as a major victory for the new league.

American Football League (AFL). Instead of joining the NFL, they would battle the established league head-on. Adams dubbed his new team the Oilers.

A CANNON SHOT

Though the NFL had some big advantages, the AFL began on solid footing. The league had committed investors and teams in large cities. Most importantly, the new league had a deal with ABC television to carry its games. Teams could use the money from the

Cannon, *center*, makes a catch before running for the only touchdown of the 1961 AFL title game.

ABC deal to recruit players that might otherwise go to the NFL. The TV deal also meant fans could easily watch the games.

The new league had another strategy to draw in fans. For years, the NFL had been a run-based league. That grinding style of football was traditional, though it was not always exciting. The AFL promised to open the field to encourage a throwing game. Billy Cannon had been a star running back for Louisiana State. Following the 1959 college season, he signed with the NFL's Los Angeles Rams. But Adams wanted Cannon to play for the Oilers and offered to double the back's salary. Adams even gave his wife's Cadillac to Cannon.

Cannon agreed to join Adams's team and the AFL. Since Cannon had a contract with the Rams, the team and the NFL sued to stop him from joining the Oilers. But they lost the lawsuit. Adams had gotten Cannon, and he gave the AFL instant credibility.

WINNING IT ALL

Cannon was one of several excellent players Adams recruited before the 1960 season. Receiver Charley Hennigan had previously tried out for a team in the Canadian Football League only to be cut. When the AFL formed, he was teaching high school biology. Still, the Oilers signed him, and he became a key target in Houston's aerial attack.

To get Cannon and Hennigan the ball, the Oilers brought in George Blanda. The colorful quarterback had spent most of the 1950s with the NFL's Chicago Bears. He threw passes and kicked field goals. After the 1958 season, legendary Bears coach George Halas told Blanda that he could no longer be the team's quarterback, just their kicker. Blanda was not interested in the offer and retired. With Houston, he would go back to doing both jobs.

The Oilers and the Los Angeles Chargers were powerhouse teams in the early years of the AFL.

The Oilers immediately excelled on the field. They debuted on September 11 against the Raiders in Oakland. In the first quarter of their first game, Blanda launched a 43-yard touchdown pass to Hennigan. The Oilers won 37–22 on their way to a 5–1 start.

No team stuck to the AFL's air-it-out plan like the Oilers. Head coach Lou Rymkus's team led the league with 3,203 passing yards in the 1960 season. Houston's 31 touchdown passes ranked second. That strong passing attack helped the Oilers go 10–4 and claim the East Division title.

The Oilers went up against the West Division champions, the Los Angeles Chargers, in the AFL Championship Game on New Year's Day 1961. It was a battle between Rymkus and his old boss turned heated rival, Chargers head coach Sid Gillman. In a hard-fought game, the Oilers took a 17–16 lead into the fourth quarter.

Early in the fourth, a Chargers' punt pinned Houston at its own 11. Two plays later, it was third-and-10 at the 12-yard line. Blanda, who had already thrown for two touchdowns, dropped back and

Quarterback George Blanda played 26 pro seasons, more than any other player.

lobbed a pass up the right sideline. It floated down into the waiting arms of Cannon near the Oilers' 35. The speedy running back took off and outran a defender who dived to try to take out his ankles. Cannon easily crossed into the end zone and ensured the Oilers a 24–16 victory.

BACK-TO-BACK

Hennigan had a solid first season in Houston. He caught 44 passes for 722 yards and six touchdowns in 1960. But he would soon break out as one of the AFL's best players.

Despite being quiet and reserved, Hennigan was hard to miss in 1961. The receiver caught 82 passes for 1,746 yards, setting a record in the young AFL. His total also surpassed the existing NFL record by nearly 300 yards. Hennigan's record would stand for another 34 years. Blanda once said of Hennigan, "No man can cover him."

"NO MAN CAN COVER HIM."
—GEORGE BLANDA ON CHARLEY HENNIGAN

Hennigan wasn't piling up empty yards, either. After a slow 1-3-1 start by the Oilers got Rymkus fired, new head coach Wally Lemm righted the ship. Starting with a 38-7 demolition of the in-state rival Dallas Texans, Houston won nine straight games to finish the season as division champions again.

In the AFL title game, Houston once again faced the Chargers, who by then had moved to San Diego. The two teams were sick of each other. They had already faced off two times in 1961.

It was not a pretty game. The teams combined for 13 turnovers. The Chargers picked off Blanda five times, while the Oilers' defense intercepted San Diego's Jack Kemp four times to go with six sacks.

Cannon (20) is chased by a Chargers defender on September 24, 1961.

Leading 3–0 in the third quarter, Houston finally put together the game's only long drive. The Oilers started at their own 20 and maneuvered to the Chargers' 35. Faced with a third-and-five, Blanda rolled out and found Cannon inside the 20-yard line. The running back fought off a tackler and raced the rest of the way to the end zone, scoring the game's sole touchdown. Despite a late San Diego field goal, Houston hung on for a 10–3 win to earn its second championship in two seasons.

INTERCEPTED

Blanda played from 1949 to 1975. No football player has competed as long as Blanda. And in 1962, he set an incredible, and dubious, record.

Houston's aerial attack was exciting. But with Blanda, it was unpredictable. That was especially true in 1962. While he threw 27 touchdown passes, he also chucked 42 interceptions, a record that still stands.

That same year, the Oilers finished 11–3 and reached the championship game for the third consecutive year. Blanda's erratic and brilliant presence was on full display against the Texans. He threw five interceptions, and the Oilers fell behind 17–0 at halftime. He then heaved a 15-yard touchdown pass to receiver Willard Dewveall in the third quarter to ignite a comeback. After Blanda's field goal in the fourth, fullback Charley Tolar rushed for a 1-yard touchdown. Blanda kicked the extra point, tying the game 17–17 and forcing overtime.

Both teams slogged through a scoreless first overtime. The game became the longest in pro football history, as it continued into a second extra session. But with 2:54 gone in the second overtime,

From 1960 to 1966, fullback Charley Tolar played for Houston. He was known as "the Human Bowling Ball."

the Texans' Tommy Brooker connected on a 25-yard game-winning field goal.

Soon after the 1962 title game loss, Houston plummeted in the standings, finishing last three straight years between 1964 and 1966. Houston rebounded in 1967 with a winning season, but it didn't last. The AFL and the NFL had decided to merge, a process that began in 1966 and became final in 1970. At that point, the 10 AFL teams joined the NFL. However, by then the Oilers' glory days of competing for championships felt like a distant memory.

The Astrodome was so difficult to make it was nicknamed "the Eighth Wonder of the World."

Oail Andrew "Bum" Phillips went 55–35 in six seasons as the Oilers' head coach.

LUV YA BLUE

The Oilers struggled in the early 1970s. Houston won only nine games between 1970 and 1973, a stretch that included a pair of back-to-back 1–13 campaigns. The team rebounded to finish 7–7 in 1974 under veteran head coach Sid Gillman.

Before the 1975 season, owner Bud Adams fired Gillman. In his place, he hired the team's defensive coordinator, Oail Andrew "Bum" Phillips. It was the start of one of the most colorful and entertaining eras of football ever enjoyed by an NFL team.

Phillips was raised in the east Texas town of Orange. True to his cowboy nature, he often roamed the sideline in blue jeans and an oversized Stetson hat. The only place he didn't wear his hat was inside the Astrodome.

When asked why, he said that his mother told him it was impolite to wear hats indoors.

He became known around the NFL for his colorful quotes. In training camp, Phillips refused to have his team play intrasquad scrimmages. "I never played Oilers against Oilers," he said. "Houston isn't on our schedule."

Oilers quarterback Dan Pastorini called Phillips the funniest coach he ever played for. But he also said Phillips was one of the

Houston quarterback Dan Pastorini jokes with Phillips before a game.

most honest. Phillips's connection with his players helped him turn the Oilers around in the late 1970s.

Houston was also stocked with talent. Pastorini was a solid quarterback. Receiver Ken Burrough was on his way to breaking Charley Hennigan's team record for career receiving yards. The defense was anchored by future Hall of Fame defensive lineman Elvin Bethea and tough linebacker Robert Brazile. Phillips put together two winning seasons in his first three years in charge. But the Oilers needed a boost to get back into the playoffs.

THE TYLER ROSE

Earl Campbell might have been the most feared running back to ever play in the NFL. At 5 feet, 11 inches and 232 pounds, Campbell was a powerhouse player. Nicknamed "the Tyler Rose" after his hometown of Tyler, Texas, Campbell ran straight ahead, and he took on anyone who dared to attempt tackling him.

After a standout college career at Texas, which ended with him winning the Heisman Trophy as college football's best player in 1977, Campbell was expected to be the top

Defensive end Elvin Bethea, *right*, played for the Oilers from 1968 to 1983 and reached the Pro Bowl seven times.

Running back Earl Campbell, *left*, rushed for more than 8,000 yards in six seasons with the Oilers.

pick in the NFL draft. The Oilers traded up to the top spot to take him. He turned out to be the missing piece of Houston's puzzle.

Just as he had in college, Campbell charged through defenders. On one famous run against the Los Angeles Rams, Campbell took a pitch from Pastorini running left. He briefly stumbled over one of his blockers in the backfield. When Campbell regained his footing, he was face-to-face with Los Angeles linebacker Isiah Robertson.

Campbell lowered his head and smashed Robertson onto his backside. Campbell then gained 10 more yards as defenders hung on. They only managed to bring Campbell down by nearly ripping his uniform off. Hard runs were Campbell's specialty. Once, when a reporter asked Phillips why Campbell seemed to get up slowly after runs, Phillips joked, "He goes down slow too."

Campbell, *right*, bowls over a would-be tackler in a game against the Los Angeles Rams.

POM-POMS AND PEP RALLIES

On November 20, 1978, the Miami Dolphins traveled to Houston for a featured *Monday Night Football* game. The Oilers distributed powder blue pom-poms to the fans in attendance. In front of a raucous, singing crowd, Campbell rushed for 199 yards and four touchdowns. His final score came on an 81-yard sprint down the right sideline. After the game,

Passionate fans celebrate their "Luv Ya Blue" Oilers.

Campbell saluted the fans for coming together and showing their blue strength.

The game is credited with kicking off the "Luv Ya Blue" era for the Oilers. The catchphrase appeared on stadium signs every week. By 1980, a country artist named Mack Hayes had turned it into a song to the tune of the Beatles' 1962 hit "Love Me Do." Riding the wave of excitement and Campbell's Rookie of the Year performance, the Oilers finished 10-6 in 1978. Houston was second to the Pittsburgh Steelers in the AFC Central Division.

After playoff wins over the Miami Dolphins and the New England Patriots, Houston traveled to Pittsburgh for the AFC title game. Pittsburgh had already won two titles in the 1970s on the back of its punishing "Steel Curtain" defensive front. The Steel Curtain made life miserable for both Pastorini and Campbell. The Oilers star rusher was held to 62 yards. Pastorini was sacked four times and threw five interceptions. The Steelers rolled to a 34–5 win.

The defeated Oilers returned to Houston. When their buses pulled into the Astrodome, the stadium was packed with singing fans. A pep rally was put on, which became a team tradition.

Fan support didn't die down in 1979. They cheered Campbell as he led the NFL in rushing yards for the second straight year. Houston improved to 11–5. However, the Oilers still weren't good

The Oilers team bus pulls into the Astrodome in January 1979, cheered on by thousands of fans.

enough to top the Steelers in the division, and the teams were on a collision course toward the AFC title game.

Just weeks earlier, Houston had beaten the Steelers 20–17 at the Astrodome. The teams met again in the AFC title game at a frozen Three Rivers Stadium in Pittsburgh. However, the Oilers came out hot. Defensive back Vernon Perry had intercepted four passes the week before in a divisional-round win over the San Diego Chargers. In the AFC title game, he picked off Pittsburgh's Terry Bradshaw in the first quarter. Perry raced 75 yards for the opening touchdown.

Despite Houston's great start, Pittsburgh held a 17–10 lead with less than two minutes to go in the third quarter. The game then turned on one of the most controversial plays in NFL history. On first-and-goal from the Pittsburgh 7, Pastorini lobbed a pass to the corner of the end zone for Mike Renfro. The second-year receiver made a spectacular leaping catch and

Wide receiver Mike Renfro, *left*, reaches for the ball in the end zone in the third quarter of the AFC title game against the Pittsburgh Steelers after the 1979 season.

dragged his feet to stay inbounds. After a long discussion, the officials said Renfro had come down out of bounds.

Phillips, wearing his trademark Stetson and a leather-and-fur coat on the sideline, was furious. Replays showed that Renfro had indeed made the catch and stayed inbounds. At the time, the NFL did not have a review system. There was nothing the Oilers could do.

Houston failed to get into the end zone again and settled for a field goal. Pittsburgh eventually won 27–13. Once again, the Oilers came home to a pep rally. Addressing the crowd, Phillips famously said, "Last year we knocked on the door. This year we beat on it. Next year we kick [it] in."

THE SNAKE

Needing a way past the Steelers, the Oilers brought in a quarterback who had beaten them before. Ken "the Snake" Stabler had led an Oakland Raiders team that had topped the Steelers in the AFC Championship Game on the way to Super Bowl XI in January 1977. After the 1979 season, the Oilers shipped Pastorini to Oakland in return for Stabler.

Stabler struggled with his new team, throwing 13 touchdowns against 28 interceptions. But Campbell enjoyed his best season yet. At that point, only one NFL player had ever rushed for 2,000 yards in a season. Campbell chased that milestone all year, ultimately finishing just 66 yards short. Still, his 13 rushing touchdowns led the NFL for the second consecutive season. However, the Oilers again came up short in the division. Both Houston and the Cleveland Browns held identical 11–5 records, but Cleveland won the division on a tiebreaker.

That meant Houston was set for a wild-card matchup with Stabler's old team, the Raiders. An October injury knocked Pastorini out for the season, so his backup, Jim Plunkett, filled his shoes in the grudge match. Plunkett completed only eight passes for Oakland, but two went for touchdowns. Meanwhile, Stabler was picked off twice. The Oilers fell to Oakland 27-7.

Linebacker Robert Brazile reached seven Pro Bowls in 10 seasons with the Oilers between 1975 and 1984.

Not long after the loss to the Raiders, Phillips and Oilers' owner Bud Adams began to feud. Thinking that the team's offense needed more support, Adams wanted to hire an offensive coordinator. Phillips disagreed, and Adams fired him. As the coach left, so did Houston's success. Without Phillips, the Oilers went 7–9 in the 1981 season. Campbell's hard-running style was quickly catching up with him.

His last 1,000-yard season came in 1983. Campbell was gone from Houston a year later and left the NFL not long after. From 1982 to 1984, the Oilers won only six games. The "Luv Ya Blue" era was officially over. It was time for a new cast of characters to bring Houston back again.

Wide receiver Ernest Givins played for the Oilers from 1986 to 1994 and left as the franchise's all-time leader in receptions and yards.

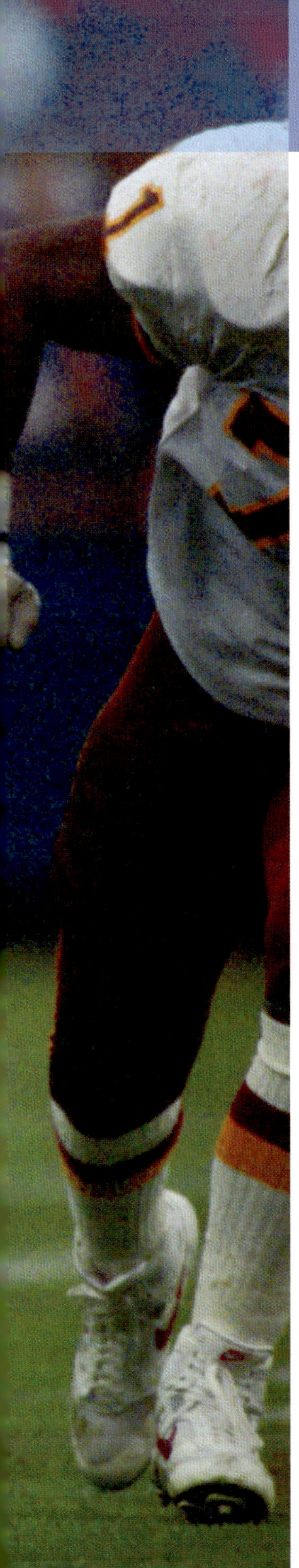

CHAPTER 4

HOUSE OF PAIN

OILERS DEFENSIVE COORDINATOR JERRY GLANVILLE RESHAPED THE TEAM when he was promoted to head coach with two games left in the 1985 season. His slogan for Houston was "Hit the beach!" The saying was inspired by US soldiers landing ashore to invade an enemy country during World War II (1939–1945). The Oilers defense would break huddles by chanting the phrase.

"HIT THE BEACH!"

—JERRY GLANVILLE

Glanville's defense seemed to enjoy crushing opponents. The Oilers became known for punishing tackles. Houston's Astrodome even earned the nickname "House of Pain."

Houston also had a spectacular offense. Deploying a strategy called "the run-and-shoot," the Oilers often lined up four wide receivers and a lone running back. Most plays were run using the shotgun formation. With this wide-open attack, Houston receivers such as Ernest Givins, Drew Hill, and Haywood Jeffires became some of the top pass catchers in team history.

Quarterback Warren Moon pulled the strings on the run-and-shoot. After starring in college at Washington, Moon had played in the Canadian Football League before signing with Houston in 1984. He possessed a powerful right arm. Former Oilers coach Bum Phillips once said that Moon could throw a football through a car wash and it would come out dry on the other side.

The Oilers finished 5–11 in Glanville's first full season in 1986. They then reached the playoffs each of the next three years. Like Phillips, Glanville was a talkative head coach. But while Phillips was jovial and well-liked by his opponents, many other NFL head coaches despised Glanville. They didn't think that Glanville's defense played hard. They thought the Oilers played dirty. After a 1987 Houston win over Pittsburgh, the Steelers' legendary head coach Chuck Noll yelled at Glanville. Noll said that Glanville's players were trying to injure his. Cincinnati Bengals head coach

Quarterback Warren Moon was inducted into the Pro Football Hall of Fame in 2006 after throwing for nearly 50,000 yards in his NFL career.

Safety Keith Bostic was a key member of the hard-hitting Oilers of the 1980s.

Sam Wyche also detested Glanville. Wyche intentionally ran up the score in a 1989 matchup against the Oilers, which Cincinnati won 61–7.

THE COLLAPSE

In the late 1980s, Houston regularly found success in the regular season. But the playoffs were another story. The Oilers lost in the divisional round after both the 1987 and 1988 seasons. In the 1989 playoffs, they faced the Steelers.

Moon threw two fourth-quarter touchdown passes to Givins as Houston rallied to take a 23–16 lead. But the Steelers tied the game in the final minute and won in overtime.

The postseason loss ended Glanville's time with Houston. His brash style had worn out its welcome. In his place, the Oilers hired Jack Pardee, who had been coaching at the University of Houston. Pardee didn't change the team's style of play at all. He had adopted

The Oilers, *in white jerseys*, fell to the Buffalo Bills in a wild-card game on January 3, 1993.

the run-and-shoot while coaching a team in the upstart United States Football League in the early 1980s. Pardee knew the offense well, and the Oilers continued to have regular-season success.

But each year, the team struggled in the playoffs. In the divisional round after the 1991 season, Houston tossed away a 21–6 lead to the Broncos and lost 26–24. But the worst was still to come.

In the wild-card round after the 1992 season, Houston traveled to Buffalo to battle the Bills. Despite the cold weather, the Oilers came out strong. Behind Moon's four touchdown passes, the Oilers took a 28–3 halftime lead. The Bills were playing behind backup quarterback Frank Reich, as their star starter Jim Kelly had been injured the week before. Early in the second half, safety Bubba McDowell intercepted Reich. McDowell's 58-yard return for a touchdown seemed to put the game away.

However, Reich slowly led the Bills back. Houston's offense began to stall. The Oilers' defense had been excellent against the pass all season. But Reich found open receivers throughout the second half against the increasingly frustrated Oilers. The Bills scored 35 straight points. Houston kicker Al Del Greco tied the game 38–38 with a late field goal. But Buffalo won in overtime. It was the worst collapse in NFL playoff history.

DISMANTLED

Oilers owner Bud Adams wanted the Astrodome to be upgraded. He had even threatened to move the team to Jacksonville in 1987. After the playoff collapse against the Bills, he told the media that unless Houston won the next year's Super Bowl, there would be big changes to the team. He even talked about moving the Oilers again. Under that pressure, Houston then started the season 1–4.

The Oilers recovered to put together an amazing 10-game winning streak and secure a division title. But not all was well with the team. On the final day of the 1993 season, the Oilers were hosting the New York Jets at the Astrodome. In the second quarter, offensive coordinator

Lineman Ray Childress racked up 53 tackles in 1993.

Buddy Ryan coached the Oilers' defense for only one season.

Kevin Gilbride and defensive coordinator Buddy Ryan started arguing. Suddenly, Ryan reached out and punched Gilbride in the face.

Players quickly broke up the scuffle. But the sight of two coaches physically fighting on the sideline shocked the NFL. It also showed the trouble going on behind the scenes in Houston. Still the team secured its 11th consecutive win, and its 12-4 record was tied for the best in the NFL.

The Oilers then took an early 10-0 lead against the Kansas City Chiefs in the playoffs. Houston still led 10-7 in the fourth quarter. But as it had before, Houston came apart late in the game. The Chiefs scored 21 fourth-quarter points and won 28-20.

Adams kept his promise to make big changes. After the season, the Oilers traded Moon. Pardee stayed on but was fired midway through a miserable 2-14 year in 1994. Another era for the Oilers was over.

SAYING GOODBYE

Following another losing season in 1995, Adams made a stunning announcement. After more than three decades in Houston, the Oilers were leaving town. Houston's refusal to update the stadium had forced his hand, he said. And he already had a new home lined up. For two years, he had been secretly negotiating with the city of Nashville, Tennessee, about relocating his team there.

The Oilers would move after the 1997 season, which meant they would spend two more years in the Astrodome. However, Houston's fans were angry and had no intention of coming to see

A Houston fan sits with a protest sign at the Astrodome in 1995.

them play. Even as the team contended for a playoff spot in 1996, its games rarely attracted fans. At the time, NFL rules stated that unless home games were sold out, they couldn't air on local TV. So, fans couldn't watch the games from home either. On top of that, more people in Tennessee than in Texas listened to the team's radio broadcasts.

The team finished 8–8. After the miserable season, the NFL gave Adams permission to move the Oilers a year early. On May 8, 1997, they officially became the Tennessee Oilers.

A NEW HOME

In Tennessee, Adams and the Oilers had a new problem. There was no good place to play. Nashville was building a brand-new stadium, but it wasn't ready yet. The "Music City" didn't have another venue fit for an NFL team. So Tennessee's other large city, Memphis, was the only choice. The team played its 1997 games in the city's Liberty Bowl. But Memphis is three hours west of Nashville, and the two cities have a long rivalry. Not many people in Memphis wanted to go see a team that was moving to Nashville in two years. A couple of the team's home games drew fewer than 18,000 fans as the team finished 8-8.

NO TO KNOXVILLE

The Oilers' other option for a temporary home after moving to Tennessee was Neyland Stadium in Knoxville. The 102,000-seat stadium is home to the University of Tennessee football team. However, Knoxville is 180 miles (290 km) east of Nashville and is not in the same time zone. Also, university officials were concerned about hosting so many college fans on Saturdays and then quickly turning around the stadium for Sunday NFL contests.

Only 30,171 fans showed up to the Liberty Bowl for the Oilers' first game in Memphis after moving from Houston.

When the team moved to Memphis, Adams had planned to stay two years. But with so few fans showing up in Memphis, the owner changed his plans again. Though the NFL didn't think Nashville's Vanderbilt Stadium was good enough for the team, the Oilers played the 1998 season there. Once again, Tennessee finished 8-8. Soon the team would have a new stadium and a new name.

Quarterback Steve McNair threw 14 touchdowns in 1997.

Running back Eddie George was one of the bright spots for the Tennessee Oilers, rushing for 1,399 yards in 1997.

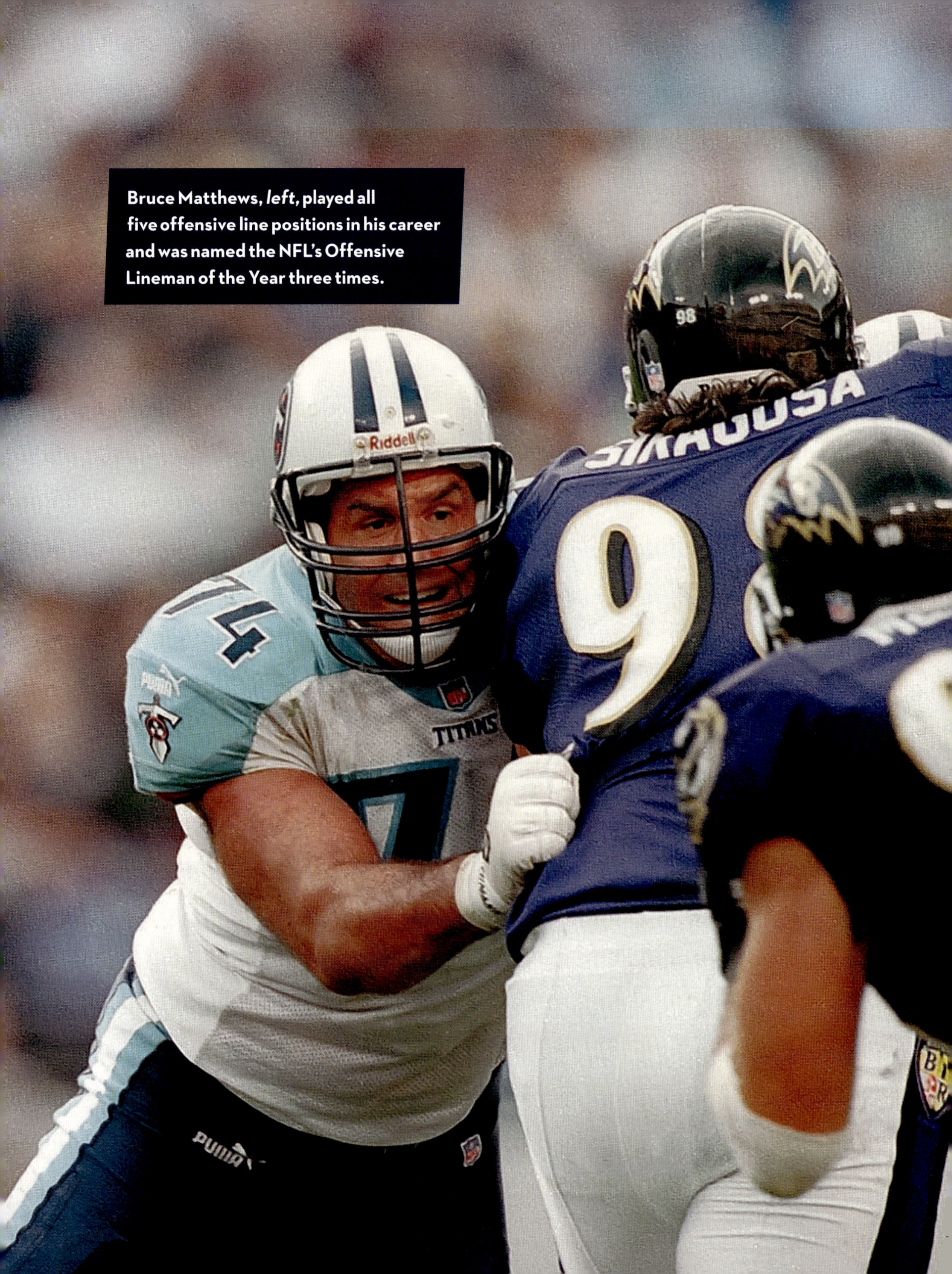

Bruce Matthews, *left*, played all five offensive line positions in his career and was named the NFL's Offensive Lineman of the Year three times.

CHAPTER 5

THE MUSIC CITY

Before the **1999** season, Bud Adams had renamed the Oilers as the Titans. On the field, fifth-year quarterback Steve McNair had established himself as a team leader. Bruising fourth-year running back Eddie George was among the best at his position. He ran behind an offensive line anchored by future Hall of Famer Bruce Matthews. The 38-year-old guard was in his 17th season with the franchise. In that time, he had rarely missed a game.

On defense, rookie defensive end Jevon Kearse took the league by storm in 1999. Known as "the Freak" for his speed and size, Kearse terrorized opposing quarterbacks. He racked up 14 1/2 sacks in the regular season and went on to win the Defensive Rookie of the Year Award. With head coach Jeff Fisher putting everything together, the Titans finished 13–3, securing second place in the AFC Central.

At their brand-new Adelphi Coliseum, the Titans hosted the Buffalo Bills for a wild-card matchup. Tennessee took a 12–0 first-half lead. However, as the clock ticked down in the fourth quarter, the Titans' lead had shrunk to just 15–13. Then the Buffalo Bills kicked a field goal

Jeff Fisher coached the Oilers/Titans from 1994 to 2010.

with 16 seconds left to take a one-point lead. The Titans would need something extraordinary to save their postseason.

Buffalo kicked off to Tennessee fullback Lorenzo Neal. He quickly handed it off to tight end Frank Wycheck at the Titans' 25-yard line. Wycheck took a few steps toward the right sideline, then spun and hurled the ball across the field. The Bills' kickoff unit had swarmed to the ball. When Tennessee receiver Kevin Dyson caught the lateral pass on the left side of the field, few defenders were near him. The crowd went from stunned to roaring as Dyson sprinted 75 yards to the end zone for a winning score. The 22–16 win instantly became known as "the Music City Miracle."

Wide receiver Kevin Dyson runs down the sideline against the Bills to complete "the Music City Miracle" on January 8, 2000.

ONE YARD SHORT

The amazing play sparked a Titans run all the way to Super
Bowl XXXIV. Even with McNair leading the Titans, they were the
ultimate underdogs against the powerful St. Louis Rams. A laid-back
man from rural Mississippi, McNair starred at tiny Alcorn State on his
way to becoming the third overall pick in the 1995 NFL Draft. As a
pro, McNair was famous for playing through pain. Injuries often kept
him from practice. But he managed to suit up every Sunday and grit
his way through games.

After the first half of the Super Bowl, Tennessee trailed 9–0.
The gutsy McNair brought his team back. George punched in a
pair of touchdowns, though the Titans missed on a third-quarter

**Running back Eddie George, *center*, rushed for 95 yards and two touchdowns in Super
Bowl XXXIV on January 30, 2000.**

George carried the ball at least 300 times in each of his eight seasons with the Oilers/Titans.

Kicker Al Del Greco drills a field goal during Super Bowl XXXIV.

two-point conversion. Then kicker Al Del Greco booted a field goal with 2:12 left to tie the game 16–16.

But the Rams immediately responded. On St. Louis's first play, quarterback Kurt Warner tossed a 73-yard touchdown pass to receiver Isaac Bruce. Behind again, McNair calmly guided Tennessee down the field. With 22 seconds left and the ball at the Rams' 27-yard line, McNair dropped back to pass. Two Rams defenders swarmed him. After managing to escape, McNair scrambled until he spotted Dyson open at the 10. Dyson's catch put Tennessee in position to tie the game with five seconds left. There was time for one more play.

The play called for Dyson to run a slant over the middle. McNair hit him with a pass at the 3-yard line. As Dyson headed for the end zone, Rams linebacker Mike Jones wrapped the receiver up and held on. Dyson tried to stretch the ball over the goal line. Instead, he came up inches short when his knee touched the ground. The game finished with a hard-fought Titans loss.

THE 2000 CLUB

The Titans' future looked bright after Super Bowl XXXIV. The team had a strong defense. It also had two rugged stars in McNair and George. The 6-foot-3, 235-pound George was a workhorse running back. In the 2000 season, he led the league with an incredible 403 carries. George and McNair guided the Titans to three playoff appearances between 2000 and 2003. However, each time the team came up short of the Super Bowl.

Dyson stretches for the goal line as St. Louis Rams linebacker Mike Jones makes the tackle on the final play of Super Bowl XXXIV.

Running back Chris Johnson's, *with football*, 2,000-yard rushing season in 2009 earned him the nickname "CJ2K."

George left the team after the 2003 season. He lasted just one more in the NFL as the toll of his physical running style caught up with him. Meanwhile, McNair's injuries worsened. In 2006, he left the Titans. McNair spent a season and a half with the Baltimore Ravens before retiring.

In 2008, the Titans found their next star runner. While Earl Campbell and George had been power backs, rookie Chris Johnson was all about speed. Coming out of college, he was timed running the 40-yard dash in a record

STEVE MCNAIR'S LEGACY

Three years after leaving the Titans, Steve McNair was shot and killed by his girlfriend. Tributes poured in for the popular player. He threw 174 touchdowns during his 13 seasons in the NFL. McNair is also remembered for running a youth football camp. In 2019, the Titans retired his No. 9 jersey. That same day, the team retired running back Eddie George's No. 27.

4.24 seconds. In his first year as a pro, Johnson blazed his way to 1,228 yards and nine rushing touchdowns. The Titans started the year 10–0 before finishing 13–3. However, Tennessee lost to the Ravens in the divisional round 13–10, with Johnson scoring the only Titans touchdown.

Johnson and the Titans started slowly in 2009. Tennessee came out of the gate 0–6. The star rusher scored only three touchdowns and was held under 100 yards four times. Then Johnson exploded. In Week 7, he rushed for 228 yards and two scores in a 30–13 win over the Jacksonville Jaguars. He then topped 100 yards every game the rest of the season. On the final day, Johnson became the sixth player to break 2,000 yards in a season. The performance earned him the NFL's Offensive Player of the Year Award. Johnson's incredible play did not lead Tennessee to the playoffs, though.

Running back Derrick Henry, *right*, fends off Jacksonville Jaguars linebacker Myles Jack while rushing for a 99-yard touchdown in December 2018.

From 2010 to 2013, Johnson rushed for more than 1,000 yards each season. But the Titans still couldn't reach the postseason.

The team lacked a good quarterback. In 2006, Tennessee had drafted highly touted Vince Young out of Texas. After his Rookie of the Year season, Young's career slowly fizzled as he battled Fisher on the sideline. In 2011, the Titans tried again, drafting Jake Locker in the first round. Locker played only four mediocre years before retiring.

BULL RUSH

Going into the 2016 draft, Tennessee had missed the playoffs for seven consecutive seasons. But the Titans drafted another stellar runner who soon helped break that streak. In the second round, the Titans selected hulking running back Derrick Henry from Alabama.

At 6 feet, 2 inches and 247 pounds, Henry was a return to the power back days of Campbell and George.

From 2016 to 2017, Henry split time with starter DeMarco Murray. They helped the Titans get back to the playoffs after the 2017 season. The next year, Henry took over full-time. And he quickly showed he was one of the league's best running backs.

Henry topped 1,000 yards for the first time in 2018. But one run captured the league's attention. On a nationally televised Thursday night game against Jacksonville, the Titans lined up for a play at their 1-yard line.

Taking the handoff, Henry picked his way through the line and then burst up the left side of the field. When a defensive back tried to slow him down, Henry used what was becoming his signature move. He reached his right arm out and stiff-armed the Jaguars defender, sending him stumbling. Henry then threw another defender to the ground while sprinting the length of the field for the first 99-yard run in the NFL since 1983. It was one of four touchdown runs on the night for the star. He finished the game with a team-record 238 yards.

A year later, Henry led the league with 1,540 rushing yards and 16 touchdowns. In the playoffs, Tennessee opened against the New England Patriots.

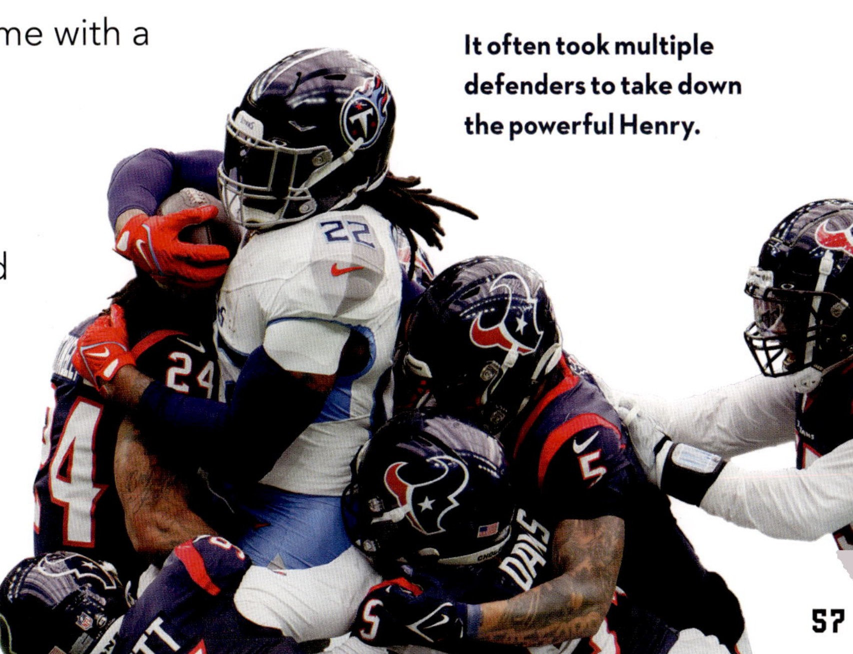

It often took multiple defenders to take down the powerful Henry.

TITANS TROPHY CASE

SUPER BOWL CHAMPIONSHIPS: 0

AFL CHAMPIONSHIPS: 2

1960, 1961

CONFERENCE CHAMPIONSHIPS: 1

1999

DIVISION TITLES: 11

AFL East: 1960, 1961, 1962, 1967
AFC Central: 1991, 1993, 2000
AFC South: 2002, 2008, 2020, 2021

All stats are through the 2024 season.

New England coach Bill Belichick had made a career out of slowing down star players, a quality that made the Patriots the NFL's most feared team for two decades. However, Henry broke through New England's strategy. On 34 punishing carries, he tallied 182 of Tennessee's 272 total yards. He also scored the winning touchdown in the third quarter. A week later against the Baltimore Ravens,

Henry left the Titans with a franchise-record 90 rushing touchdowns.

Henry bulldozed his way to 195 rushing yards on 30 carries. But he made his biggest play with his arm. In the third quarter, he took a direct snap from the center. After faking a run up the middle, he stopped and lobbed the ball to receiver Corey Davis for a 3-yard touchdown. Tennessee won the game 28–12. The next week, the Titans fell to the Kansas City Chiefs, who went on to win the Super Bowl.

Tennessee rode Henry's 2,000-yard season back to the playoffs in 2020, where they faced the Ravens again in the wild-card round. Baltimore held Henry to just 40 yards rushing. The Titans lost 20–13. A year later, the Titans' ground game was smothered by the Cincinnati Bengals as Tennessee lost 19–16 in the divisional round.

Henry stayed in Tennessee through the 2023 season, but never reached the playoffs again. As he and other stars left, the team slipped in the standings. The Titans were entering another new era. And the team's fans hoped they would see a new generation of stars take over.

TIMELINE

The Oilers are one of eight teams to make up the new AFL. After finishing 10-4 in the regular season, Houston wins the first AFL championship by beating the Los Angeles Chargers 24-16.

1960

Despite 42 interceptions by quarterback George Blanda, the Oilers reach the AFL Championship Game for the third year in a row. They lose 20-17 to the Dallas Texans in double overtime on December 23.

1962

Houston reaches the AFC title game for a second straight year but once again falls to the Steelers on January 6.

1980

1961

The Oilers repeat as champions by beating the San Diego Chargers 10-3 in the AFL championship.

1975

Houston promotes defensive coordinator Bum Phillips to head coach.

1979

The "Luv Ya Blue" Oilers reach the AFC title game but lose to the Pittsburgh Steelers 34-5 on January 7.

1985

Houston hires Jerry Glanville as head coach with two games left in the season. He leads the team to the playoffs each year between 1987 and 1989.

Bud Adams announces his decision to move the team to Nashville, Tennessee.

1995

Titans running back Chris Johnson becomes the sixth player to surpass 2,000 yards rushing in a single season.

2009

Henry becomes the eighth running back in NFL history to surpass 2,000 yards in a season after rushing for a franchise-record 250 on the final day of the season.

2020

1993

On January 3, the Oilers throw away a 35–3 lead and eventually lose 41–38 in overtime to the Buffalo Bills in the wild-card round.

2000

On the strength of "the Music City Miracle," the Titans reach the Super Bowl for the first time. They lose 23–16 to the St. Louis Rams after Kevin Dyson is tackled at the 1-yard line with time expiring on January 30.

2018

Derrick Henry pulls off a 99-yard touchdown run in a game against the Jacksonville Jaguars.

backfield—the set of players, including quarterback and running backs, who line up behind the offensive line.

contract—an agreement to play for a certain team.

coordinator—an assistant coach who is in charge of the offense, defense, or special teams.

debut—first appearance.

draft—a system that allows teams to acquire new players coming into the league.

era—a period of time in history.

franchise—an entire sports organization.

interception—a pass that is caught by a defensive player.

investor—a person who provides money for businesses.

lateral—a pass that goes sideways or backward.

merge—join with another to create something new, such as a company, a team, or a league.

postseason—another word for playoffs; the time after the end of the regular season when teams play to determine a champion.

retire—to end one's career.

rival—an opponent with whom a player or team has a fierce and ongoing competition.

rookie—a professional athlete in his or her first year of competition.

sack–a tackle of the quarterback behind the line of scrimmage before he can pass the ball.

shotgun–a formation in which the quarterback lines up 5 to 7 yards behind the center and takes the snap in the air.

turnover–loss of the ball to the other team through an interception or fumble.

underdog–the person or team that is not expected to win.

veteran–someone who has played for many years.

ONLINE RESOURCES

To learn more about the Tennessee Titans, please visit **abdobooklinks.com** or scan this QR code. These links are routinely monitored and updated to provide the most current information available.

INDEX